BE
LIKE
TEFLON

JASLEEN
KAUR

Co-Editors	Catriona Duffy and Lucy McEachan, Panel
Graphic Design	Åbäke
Text	Jasleen Kaur and Amanprit Sandhu
Copy Editing	Kaite Welsh
Printed by	J Thomson Colour Printers
Paper	G.F Smith
Published by	Glasgow Women's Library and Dent–De–Leone

Jasleen would like to thank all those who contributed to the conversations in this book: Elmira 'Bolly' Fauchon, Mireille Fauchon, Amanroop Kaur, Harbhajan Kaur, Jaswant Kaur, Edna Paes, Nikita Paes and Ram Singh.

Her thanks are extended to Catriona Duffy, Lucy McEachan, Margie Orford, Amanprit Sandhu and Kajsa Ståhl for adding their voices.

Printed in Scotland
Edition of 750

Be Like Teflon
is kindly supported by
Creative Scotland and is
produced by Panel

www.wearepanel.co.uk

Glasgow Women's Library
23 Landressy Street
Glasgow G40 1BP
UK

www.womenslibrary.org.uk

ISBN
978–0–9522273–1–1

Dent–De–Leone
48 Wilton Way
London E8 1BG
UK

www.dentdeleone.com

ISBN
978–1–907908–52–1

FROM
GLASGOW
WOMEN'S
LIBRARY

CREATIVE SCOTLAND

ALBA | CHRUTHACHAIL

Glasgow Women's Library is a 'Recognised Collection of National Significance' and the only Accredited Museum in the UK dedicated to women's lives, histories and achievements. The Library has been providing information, resources and services since 1991, through its lending library, archive collections and innovative programmes of public events and learning opportunities.

Panel is a curatorial practice founded in 2010 and led by Catriona Duffy and Lucy McEachan. Based in Glasgow, Panel celebrates design in relation to particular histories, archives and collections through exhibitions, events and commissions.

Åbäke is a transdisciplinary graphic design collective, founded in 2000 by Patrick Lacey, Benjamin Reichen, Kajsa Ståhl and Maki Suzuki in London, after meeting at the Royal College of Art. Much of their work concentrates on the social aspect of design and the strength that collaboration can bring to a project.

Jasleen Kaur (b.1986, Glasgow) is an artist currently living and working in London. Her work is an ongoing exploration into the malleability of culture and the layering of social histories within the material and immaterial things that surround us. Her practice examines the hierarchy of histories and labour using a range of mediums and methods including sculpture, video, conversation and cooking.

Amanprit Sandhu works as a curator in London. Her ancestral home is the Punjab, in pre-partitioned India. An occasional writer, she is interested in South Asian story telling, historical accounts and biographies; personal truths, fictions and the potential of tall stories.

A RECİPE
FOR A BOOK

4 pages Nuclear Acid,
32 pages Champagne,
24 pages Milk,
32 pages Lavender,
40 pages Harvest

All together

Be Like Teflon by Jasleen Kaur is one of a series of
limited-edition products developed by curatorial
practice Panel with Glasgow Women's Library.

Collectively titled *From Glasgow Women's Library*
and made in a series of partnerships between
artists and manufacturers, each product is
inspired by the organisation, it's library, archive
and museum collection. In this way, they speak
to women's history and experience, exploring
ideas that uncover, sample and reference the
diverse and unsung stories that Glasgow Women's
Library holds. The Library is a unique resource in

Scotland, housing a huge collection of materials by, for and about women, all donated by users, supporters, members and publishers.

Drawing upon a practice of questioning hierarchies of culture, history and labour through the art of cooking, Jasleen's research focused upon the Library's collection of cookery books, and upon the voices and recipes that she found missing. In developing a product for *From Glasgow Women's Library*, she found a need for a new recipe book that could foreground lost or under-represented experience and that could use acts of communal cooking to ask questions: Whose stories count? Who speaks for whom?

And so, *Be Like Teflon* harvests women's voices. In a collection of conversations between Jasleen and women of Indian heritage living in the UK, arise themes of labour, duty, sustenance and loss. This book finds a place for their histories, experience and strength. It makes them visible. Through the simple act of listening, over a hot tava or plate of food, begin acts of solidarity and self-nourishment.

WHAT ARE YOU FEEDING YOURSELF?

Dr. Karen Salt asks at a
Women of Colour Index
Reading Group.[1]

At the age of sixteen or seventeen I developed
bulimia. A means of shrinking, disappearing,
a slow suicide.

1. I find myself in at the time of writing.

To ask yourself, 'What you are feeding yourself?'
— physically, spiritually — strikes me hard, deep
in my belly, in my gut. This self-destruction,
performed for almost half my life, was a way of
coping, an accomplished ritual, used to block
out a feeling, a memory, a betrayal. It was an
unconscious frenzy to fill a void, to then spill out
violently the contents of my body, till numbness
was restored. Now healing, I wonder if resisting
nourishment was a silent scream for help —
a hunger strike, a protest. I'm still trying to
understand it, as I carefully pummel roasted jeera
seeds, knead my fists into atta, peel the skin from
a roast batao.

This book began out of silence and smallness,
of a desperation to find my voice and body.
These pages are an act of self-nourishment, self-
preservation and survival. Amongst my hand-
scrawled notes from the reading group I read,
'How do we research survival/ how does survival
become research?'

I needed to hear the voices of women in my life,
I needed to prepare meals and eat with them. This
project makes room for us, it makes us visible.
It began intuitively, by having conversations
with women I know, with a shared heritage and

experience. As I was having these conversations, listening and transcribing them, I was not anticipating what would be dredged up from the pits and past of my own life. An anxiety-inducing lack. Lack of closeness with the women in my family, of things spoken, of truth, of agency. I have learned that abuse fractures relationships well beyond the abuser and victim. That in producing generations of dutiful daughters and housewives to marry Sikh men before thirty, we replicate silence. And that fathers and brothers come first, speak last and always will. Unprepared for the unprocessed adolescent trauma buried in me, I took time out from this project and returned when I was ready again.

At the time of writing I am reading more than ever and finding strength in women's words. I read Urvashi Butalia's *The Other Side of Silence: Voices from the Partition of India* — at last a woman's voice! Her research foregrounds the unheard voices of women, amidst violent, colonial, geo-political decision making, which resulted in mass migration. Fourteen million people living along newly founded religious lines were displaced. Learning about this is harrowing enough, let alone how this history plays out in acts of violence on the bodies of women.

13

Rape, murder, suicide. She talks about the
difference and difficulties of interviewing women
when husbands and sons were around; 'they
tend to take over the interview, inadvertently or
otherwise, making women lapse into a sort of
silence.' Butalia's book speaks from the margins.
Different to any other books, films, talks or
exhibitions on the subject of the partition of
India (almost always authored by men) these
testimonies are truthful and traumatic, they scar
and heal. I try to make sense of how abuse has
been allowed to happen, how it is normalised and
talked or not talked about. I remember my dad
telling me of his friends back home, two brothers,
who at the time of Partition killed their wives and
daughters to protect them from being abducted
or raped. 'This is izzat,' my dad says. I can't help
but parallel Butalia's book of testimonies with
the stories of women in my own family, their
continual silencing and removal — all for izzat?
I buy multiple copies and gift them to female
family members.

Between seven and nine o'clock every evening,
my mum would cook roti for the family and
I learned from watching her daily how to roll
and turn a ball of dough simultaneously into
a perfect round, how to transform a cup of old

dhal into a second meal of dhal wale roti, how
to cook for twenty-five people with the help of a
sister, how to do the food shop when your bank
balance is anaemic and how to cook for strength.
I remember my biji visiting from India, making
gobi paratha for lunch, then using the leaves to
make sabji for dinner — a clue to how financially
strained her life had been at times.[2] Most women
close to me have lived tough lives, growing up
you could sense it; the absence of an auntie or a
sister (only visible in photographs, their names no
longer mentioned in households), a forced smile
to detract from an ill-tempered husband, a bitten
tongue, or a turned-off hearing aid when the other
cheek couldn't be turned. Along with good round
rotia, you learn all this too. I wonder if Mum
turning vegan seven years ago was also an act
of resistance, not to the meat industry, but to the
men in the house. Defying her familial duties and
cooking separate meals to nourish primarily her
body.

2. As a young boy, sometimes Biji would tell my
   dad to go around the houses with a bowl, asking
   for some spare atta. With all the spares Biji would
   be able to make some roti for the family.

It is both an inherited and personal trauma that drives this book. An acknowledgement of the silences, what is not said and not heard, the silencing of women in my life and, as I learn, in my cultural history too. A whole heritage of mistreatment, voicelessness and disempowerment, repeated again and again by a patriarchal force that keeps us quiet.

Whether it's around a kitchen table or from the pages of a book, hearing the voices of resilient women is like having the companionship of a sister or mother — tender and sustaining, like maha di dhal on a sodden wet day in Glasgow. With that innate knowledge of measuring by eye, atta, chawal, mirch, comes the wisdom of a woman's experience, as she tells us to, 'be like teflon, be like teflon, don't let anything stick.' [3]

3. As told to Amanroop by her mother-in-law.

THE

CON–
VERSATÏONS

What follows are the transcriptions of four conversations between Jasleen Kaur and women in her life with a shared heritage and experience. They have been recorded by Jasleen and within each she is called **Me** and others are named as Jasleen calls them.

Each transcription is accompanied by recipes and by a list of the people in the conversation. Through indication of immediate and extended family tags and titles, their place in the conversation, and in geography and history, is signposted and can be referenced as each transcription is read.

As with all conversations, whether around a table, in front of the TV, travelling by car, or preparing food, the voices occupy different spaces, some loudly present, some quietly distant. And so, set vertically in columns across the page, here, each voice is given its own space, anchored by the speaker's name at the top — always present, always visible.

Me: Mum:

YOU JUST MADE DO.

Mum: Jasleen's mother

Dad: Jasleen's father

Granny: Jasleen's maternal grandmother,
also referred to as 'Mum'
by Jasleen's mother

Grandad: Jasleen's maternal grandfather,
also referred to as 'Dad'
by Jasleen's mother

Onkar (Bitu): Jasleen's maternal uncle

Nita: Jasleen's maternal aunt

Veera: Jasleen's maternal aunt

Kuldip: Jasleen's maternal aunt

Me: Mum:

In my mum's car on her way to work at Bensons for Beds, Glasgow. She is dropping me off halfway to get a bus to Granny's house. The conversation feels forced, she feels uncomfortable, we don't have these types of conversations often. The sound of the car engine and tyres on the road hum in the background. She has a cold.

Who taught you to cook? How did you learn to cook if you didn't get taught?

When I was young, 'cause I was the eldest of five and Mum and Dad were out at work, they used to give me certain responsibilities. This was in Glasgow, so maybe when I was about eleven or twelve. I had to maybe just prep some stuff before they came home, even if it was just to make the atta. And then I would help Mum when she got home, give her a hand, so that's how I picked up how to cook.

IT'S ALSO HOW I LEARNED TO COOK.

What else would you prep?

Me:	Mum:

Maybe just prep some vegetables and that. I don't really remember that much, I used to make the atta and the roti, I learned to make the roti when I was about twelve…twelve, thirteen. So Dad used to cook quite a bit then as well. We used to eat quite a bit of meat so usually I would give him a hand, washing it and that, when he came home. Lamb, chicken or something.

What time would your mum and dad get back from work?

Usually it'd be about six, after six o'clock. And obviously I would be responsible for looking after my siblings as well.

What would Granny cook?

She'd usually make, like, sabjis, like gobi and bataou and dhals and stuff.

So just like now.

Yeah, except we used to do more

Me: Mum:

---

meat cooking in those days, maybe
twice a week.

Where did you buy all the ingredients, where could you buy masala and stuff?

That's something I don't really
remember. Possibly they just picked
it up from one of the cash 'n' carry's
or one of the few Asian food grocers
that were around in those days. I don't
really recall. We didn't have Asda
and Safeway back in those days. It's
something maybe your granny will
be able to answer better 'cause I just
remember we used to go to, like, John
Curley's, to go and get the bread rolls.
That was like a delicatessen selling
sliced meats.

Where did you live at that point?

We lived in a tenement flat.

How many rooms? Do you remember it?

We had three rooms, one was Granny
and Grandad's room and one was like

Me: **Mum:**

---

a living room with a wee recessed area where the bed was and there was a kitchen with a recessed area as well.

Who slept in the living room?

I think Bitu must have slept in the living room. Nita and Veera were small, they were in Granny and Grandad's room — Nita definitely 'cause they had two beds lined up. And I think myself and Auntie Kuldip were in the other room — you just made do. This was in Springburn, Hawthorn Street. It was a really rough area, a lot of slums, it's all changed now, a lot of slums, youngsters just hanging around outside. This was probably early '70s...yeah probably early '70s 'cause I think was 1973 or '74 when we moved to Bearsden.

Were there other Asians in that area?

Not in Springburn, no. Most of the Asian people lived in those days in the west end of Glasgow, around Charing Cross way. People who had

Me: Mum:

---

their own houses, they would have been in Bishopbriggs and that.

What was your favourite meal when you were growing up and what about now?

We used to make silly things like, erm [laughing] —I don't know if Granny invented this — we used to mix Rice Krispies with Nestlé Cream, and I don't know what else we used to put in it but it turned into a big crunchy mess! Gooey, not a dessert but, I don't know...we used to eat it with a spoon. We used to add other things to it, but it was always Rice Krispies with Nestlé Cream and I don't know what else.

What's Nestlé Cream?

Nestlé Cream is just like really, really condensed, thick, thick cream.

Like condensed milk?

No, condensed milk is a wee bit more runny. This was just like, you could

Me:	Mum:

---

cut through this almost. It's a bit like quark, even thicker. I think we used to make things with it, or use it, thinking cream was so good you know. We used it for cooking or just as a dessert. We used to buy packs and packs of it at the cash 'n' carry — packs of biscuits, packs of Nestlé Cream.

What cash 'n' carry was it? One owned by apne?

Don't think so, I wouldn't have really picked up on that in those days. We didn't really have a lot of our own friends back in those days, the only apne we used to see was near our cousins.

Did you like eating sabjia and stuff or did you start eating different foods?

Well we did obviously eat a lot of other foods too, goray things, like cheese toast, beans and tinned soups, mostly at lunch time — you know you get those Knorr packets of soups

Me: Mum:

---

that are dried, we used to use them a lot. We used to eat meat pies and rolls with cold meat in them.

Do you have memories of India?

No I don't.

But you were seven when you came over?

I must have blanked them all out because of the big change. I don't remember any of it.

Do you remember what yous ate at your wedding?

Just Langar… I can't remember what we ate or what was cooked, it was just, 'somebody make the Langar.' It wasn't involved like, you know, like nowadays. Nowadays you go and decorate the Gurdwaras and all that and decide on the food — there was nothing like that. I was a very naïve seventeen-year-old. Although I went to school and got a job and

everything, I wasn't like, I wasn't very
streetwise and didn't really…I knew
the way into town and all that but,
'cause we didn't really mix and
didn't have a lot of friends, we didn't
talk and get to know other people's
viewpoints and things.

**Did you have your own thoughts? That
sounds like a really daft question, like did
you get angry with Granny?**

Yeah! Yeah, yeah.

[We arrive at the bus stop]

Right, is this Sheildhall Road?

I think it must be.

INGREDIENTS

2 tablespoons vegetable oil
½ teaspoon mustard seeds
½ teaspoon cumin
2 medium onions, chopped
3–4 cloves garlic, crushed
2-inch fresh ginger root, peeled and grated
1–2 green chillies, finely chopped
250g carrots, chopped (5–6 qty)
4 medium potatoes
1 large sweet potato
1 cup peas, frozen
1 teaspoon haldi
1 teaspoon salt
1 teaspoon garam masala
Bunch of fresh methi (fenugreek), chopped

METHOD

Heat the oil and add the mustard seeds till they pop, then add the cumin seeds. Add the onion, garlic and chillies. Sauté for a few minutes, adding the spices along with the methi. Cook for a minute before adding the carrots, cook for a further 5 minutes then add the potato.

INGREDIENTS

2 tablespoons vegetable oil
½ teaspoon mustard seeds
2 medium onions, finely chopped
4 cloves garlic
3-inch fresh ginger root, peeled and grated
2 green chillies
1 teaspoon haldi
½ teaspoon ground coriander
½ teaspoon ground cumin
1 teaspoon salt
1 tomato, finely chopped
2 tins chickpeas, drained
300g fresh spinach, chopped

METHOD

Prepare the tadka by heating the mustard seeds in oil till they pop. Add garlic, onions, ginger and chillies until lightly sautéed. Then add the spices and chopped tomato. Cook for a minute or so before adding the chickpeas. Mix to coat well with the seasoned tadka. Finally add the spinach* and cook on low heat for 10–15 minutes. Garnish with chopped fresh coriander and serve with Indian breads or rice.

*Add ½ cup of water to make a moist curry

*THAT'S
HOW
HARÐ
WE
WORKEÐ
BACK THEN.*

Granny: Jasleen's maternal grandmother

Grandad: Jasleen's maternal grandfather

Mum: Jasleen's mother

Poono: Granny's paternal aunt,
also referred to as 'Chachi'

Taya: Granny's (oldest) paternal uncle

Mummy: Granny's mother

Bhai Ji: Granny's father, also referred
to as 'Dad' by Granny

Chacha: Granny's paternal uncle

Auntie Kuldip: Granny's daughter, Jasleen's maternal aunt

Jaswant: Granny's daughter, Jasleen's mother

Onkar (Bitu): Granny's son, Jasleen's maternal uncle

Pritam: Granny's sister

Gurbhagat: Granny's brother

Veera: Granny's daughter, Jasleen's maternal aunt

Nita: Granny's daughter, Jasleen's maternal aunt

Mama: Grandad's maternal uncle

Me: Granny: Grandad:

At Granny's house in Crossmyloof Gardens, Glasgow whilst eating a lunch of yellow dhal, soya chunk sabji, buckwheat, dahi and spiralised courgette salad. Granny, Grandad and I are sitting at the dining room table. In the background are the sounds of metal spoons on melamine plates, eating sounds, the washing machine whirring and a man on the Indian TV channel loudly reciting Sukhmani Sahib prayers. I am speaking to them in English and they reply in Punjabi.

Grandad is suffering from dementia.

I was talking to Mum in the car about when you were younger. I was asking if she had any memories, of like, I was asking her, 'who taught you to cook?' She said that before you got back from the shop, she'd prepare the atta.

Yes she used to knead the atta, and she used to the do the cleaning too. Grandad would make the sabji when he got in.

What else would she do?

She did all the cleaning.

35

Me: Granny: Grandad:

She would do all the cleaning.

She did everything.

WHEN WE WERE YOUNG, MUM WAS
QUITE STRICT ABOUT HOUSEWORK —
EVERY DAY THE LIVING ROOM WOULD
BE POLISHED AND HOOVERED AND THE
SOFAS WHACKED WITH A TEA TOWEL TO
GET RID OF THE DUST AND FLUFF THEM
UP — I DON'T REMEMBER THE LAST
TIME I POLISHED MY FURNITURE, OR
OWNED POLISH.

Would she make the tarka or would
Grandad do that?

Grandad would do that.

Did you not cook?

Me, I used to do other things, wash
the clothes, press the clothes and do
other jobs.

So Grandad would do all the...

No, I used to make the roti.

Me: Granny: Grandad:

Okay, and Grandad would make all the sabjia.

Yes he'd make the sabjia soobjia. I'd do any clothes that needed washing, pressing, those kinds of jobs.

Who taught you to cook, Granny? Kinnae sikhaia?

Me? When we were in India we used to live together with our chachi and taya and, out of all my sisters, I did the most work with my chachi. We used to make dinner for the whole household, right, I'd do a lot with my chachi. Then at seventeen I got married and I had to do a lot of work, because the family was much bigger when I got married.

Did you move in with Grandad's family?

Yes.

Did you have a Doli as well?

Yes, so many people came, from the

boys side a lot of people came. They came from quite far away — Rhaniya. Back then, we used to cover our faces. When you did the Anand Karaj, your face would be covered, right?

With a chooni? So you didn't know who you were going to marry?

No.

No. I don't know why, it must have been the way things were back then. It didn't need to be that way though. This is very good, [referring to the spiralised courgette salad] we'll make this twice a week, right? [to Grandad]

Did you have Langar at your wedding?

Yes, the Langar was at home, the house was very big and open. Girls looked at your grandad and were surprised. Honestly! [we laugh out loud] They said, 'very handsome!' You know, when they see the boy's side arriving? Nowadays you know what he looks like.

Me: Granny: Grandad:

Were you the first to get married in the family?

No, no. First my taya's daughters got married, then my older sister. After that, me.

Did your mum teach you to cook?

I learned from my chachi. We used to do a lot of housework like sorting the bedding, that kind of work, I did it with her.

Were you close with her?

Hmm.

What was her name?

I've forgotten everything, Poono, it was Poono. She used to pray as well. This is very tasty, I really like it.

Did you go to school, Granny?

Yes, I went to school. At my school we used to learn cooking actually.

Me: Granny: Grandad:

There'd be a table there and we'd gather
the ingredients in baskets and then put
all the ingredients in the pots and pans
and then Miss would come and see
what we'd made.

What would you make?

Like, kheer khoor and other things,
like chaat. We'd take the ingredients to
school and then bring the dishes home
with us.

Just like we did.

Is that right? [laughing]

**We called it Home Economics. We'd take
fifty pence, they'd buy all the ingredients,
everyone cooked it in pairs, then we would
split the food and take it home.**

We'd leave the house early in the
morning and pass Bhai Ji's shop, he had
a cycle repair shop in Moga. So first, in
the morning, we'd take him roti before
we went to school, drop it off to him
and walk to school straight from there.

Me: Granny: Grandad:

What would he have for lunch? Sabji?

I don't remember, Mummy would
make it — paratha or sabji or
something like that. We used to have
our clothes washed outside the house,
Dad would say, 'my daughters, I'll
keep them like boys.' There were five
of us, 'I'm going to educate my girls
a lot.' He used to study and we used
to study. We'd get up at seven o'clock,
our grandad didn't like it, that we
went to school to study. I'd get up at
seven o'clock to go to school and he'd
say, 'no, do the housework.' My older
sister studied up to Year Ten, I studied
up to Year Seven, till sixteen years
old. He'd say, 'you're not studying any
more, get them married.'

But your dad wanted you to study?

Yes he wanted that, because he'd
left India when we were very young.
When he came to Glasgow we were
very young and he'd send money for
us to get married.

Me: Granny: Grandad:

You know your kitchen in India, was it on the ground?

> Yeah, it was on the ground, small like this size, [points to mark out a space about 2m x 1m] in my chachi's kitchen. In the morning we'd fetch the milk from the cows, for making butter or drinking lassi. That's the kind of work we'd do, I was very strong.

Did you used to milk the cows?

> Yeah, we kept cows for milking.

Did you eat meat there?

> No, no, sometimes my chacha would, but we didn't eat meat there. Here we did everything because of my dad — go to different shops and eat pie-a-pooi-a and everything!

What would you eat for breakfast in Punjab?

> We would've eaten parathay.

Me: Granny: Grandad:

I made missi roti the other day.

Really, how did you make them?

We just had them with plain yellow dhal. I made them with besan, methi...

You would have put onions in, right?

Yeah. Did Mum go to school in India?

No, no, later, when we came here.

So she didn't speak any English until she came here?

She learnt it here. [To Grandad] She didn't learn there did she? I don't remember.

She was seven she said.

Aha? She would have started school then.

She said she can't remember anything from India.

Me:	Granny:	Grandad:

I don't remember. Slowly, slowly I
forget more and more...

**And, what age would Auntie Kuldip have
been, like one, two?**

She must have been two years.

When you moved here?

Kuldip...Kuldip sach, was born
earlier in '65. Aho, first Jaswant, then
Onkar, then Kuldip, she was young.

**So you moved in '67, so she was born in
'65, is that right?**

Yes, she was two-years-old then. I
came with your mum, I don't know
how we managed to come over, I
don't know, honestly. [laughing]

**You know when you moved here, did you
miss India?**

That's why we went to the police
so many years after, about four, five
years after, I don't know how many

years after. First Pritam went to the
police...

Ten years after.

Ten years after. We said, 'either send
us back or...say that our father has
called us over...'

You weren't happy here?

Aha, we weren't happy.

Why?

Grandad used to get angry, he'd say,
'I'm going to complain, I'm going
to go the police.' Grandad wanted
us to become official, right — how
long will we wander around like this,
right? At first Bhai Ji would get us
free milk for the children, the kids
got it for free, then Bhai Ji got it all
stopped.

Why did he stop that?

He said, 'if someone finds out then

they'll send you back.' He didn't used
to give us any money, right, for the
children, he didn't give us anything,
right. Grandad used to kick up a fuss
every day, he'd say, 'I'm going to the
police today to tell them.' And I'd
say, 'no don't tell them, no don't tell
them.' Then first Pritam went to the
police, right. They told them that,
'our father has called us over...' The
police looked at their passports and
sent them home. They told us, 'you
should do this too.' We thought to
ourselves, 'it's happened for them
fine, we should do it too.'

So then I went to the police station,
told them that our father had called
us over, that our passports and
everything were with Bhai Ji.

Did he get in trouble from the police?

Who? No, no! We told them he takes
the money from us, makes a home for
himself, and us, it's very difficult for
us. The police couldn't do anything
about the money.

Me: Granny: Grandad:

So he lived separately?

Hah. When Grandad used to do
work for Bhai Ji, he used to hand
over all our money to Bhai Ji. That's
how Bhai Ji could afford to keep
buying houses. Our house was rented
and even then, he would come over
whenever he wanted to and say, 'I'll
take what little rent you can pay, if
you can't pay it all.'

Do you think he was greedy?

Aho! You know what, when he
first called us over it was different,
everything happened when Gurbhagat
came. When Nita was born he used
to say, 'there's no need for you to
work, we'll do it ourselves you stay at
home.' In the morning I'd stay quiet
and say, 'hah, hah,' Nita was only
three weeks, and without saying a
word I'd go to the shop.

Three weeks old?

Hah, as well as that, on the way to the

Me: Granny: Grandad:

---

shop I'd drop Veera to school. I did a
lot of hard work, myself.

**Because you had no money you went
to work?**

Hah, what else? We needed the
money. We also hoped we could have
a home one day.

**So the money you made from the shop,
you didn't give it to Bhai Ji?**

No, not then, at first we did, we gave
him whatever we had to give him. But
not then.

**How much money would you make in a
day?**

Forty-five pounds a week.

Forty-five pounds?

Forty-five pounds a week.

A week?

At first we only got five pounds a
week. When we had to give them
money we would save up all our
pennies. They'd come everyday, Bhai
Ji and Gurbhagat right. Then one day,
the money we made in the holidays,
we gave it all to them and said,
'please go, we put our hands together
in front of you, we will be fine, you
mean nothing to us any more, take
the money, now don't come back to
our house again.'

You said that to them?

Aho. Every day they'd come and
annoy us and ask for their money,
after our rent we had very little
money. Then they left us alone,
they left us alone and we stopped
speaking. Then we became official,
I went to the police and told them
that when we came here, that Bhai
Ji kept our passports, we don't claim
anything.

**So was the shop and everything under
Bhai Ji's name?**

No, when we started renting the shop,
he said, 'I'm not coming with you to
be your guarantor.' He said, 'I'm not
coming with you if you're going to open
a bank account.'

Where was the shop again?

Park Road, we got it ourselves. Then, I
used to go to the shop by myself, drop
Veera to school, take Nita with me and I
had one goree girl helping me a little bit.

So she spoke English to the customers?

Yeah, whatever little English I could
speak, I spoke. We learnt some from
working at Bhai Ji's shop. And then in
the evening Grandad would work, after
school Onkar would work and if we had
to go to the cash 'n' carry on the way
home, or if Grandad went, we'd bring
the stock back on the bus. That's how
hard we worked back then.

What was your Park Road shop called?

[correcting me] Parkhead.

Me:	Granny:	Grandad:

Parkhead?

Hmm.

It was called Bargain Store, our first shop. It was a small shop, this size [using her arms to indicate the size in the room], this size right? With a storeroom at the back. Then on Park Road we got a bit bigger shop. Then when Onkar left school he said, 'get an even bigger shop, that'll be better.' Then we got another Bargain Store, the big one. All hardware shop businesses. We did a lot of hard work.

How did you look after Nita?

I just did. Then in the evening we'd take the bus home.

Did you always cook sabji at night? Roti-sabji?

Hah, we didn't have a lot to eat, we cooked a little.

So what would you cook that was cheap?

Me: Granny: Grandad:

Where did you buy, like, you know we go to Morrisons and you can buy like haldi, garam masala, dhal...

There weren't shops like that then.

Did you like the food here, cheese and all that?

Back then we ate everything.

Would you make it on a tava, cheese toast?

Hah. At Langside we ate a lot of cheese-choose, egg-oog, we ate everything then, you know.

Was egg bhurji something you made in India, or something you made here?

Aha! We never made it there, we'd eat that here. This is the way our story goes. Goray lived like this as well, in small houses. This is the way it was at first, wages were little, costs were high.

52

Me: Granny: Grandad:

Grandad how did you learn to cook, if Granny is saying you used to cook in the house?

He was eleven when he started cooking.

Really?

He was with his mama. They didn't bother that the boys left home to do work, you know.

Why did Grandad cook here, because you were busy?

Here, he had to do it, didn't he? He'd say, 'I'll do this, you do something else, I'll make the sabji.' He used to cook meat, you know, and if the kids were helping him, I'd do some other work.

Like cleaning the house?

Yeah, the children would help him and I'd do that.

Me: Granny: Grandad:

What's your favourite sabji?

That I don't know, they are all good.
Then, we didn't have karelay karoolay,
you didn't get all the different
vegetables and things like that, we'd
just use the sabjia we'd get locally.
Like aloo muttar gajjar and things like
that.

Bataou and things like that?

You didn't get aubergines then.

No probably not. You know what we had the other day, pakoria sabji.

Oh pakoria, do you want to take some
with you? I've had some made.

Do you just boil them in the taree?

No you fry the tarka first, then you add
vadi — have you got vadia? They're
round shaped, take them from me. You
fry the vadi then add some aloo. Take
some more pakoray from me. The sabji
turns out very nice, very nice.

INGREDIENTS

2 tablespoons vegetable oil
1 teaspoon cumin seeds
3 cloves garlic, finely chopped
1 onion, diced
1-inch fresh ginger root, peeled and grated
1 teaspoon turmeric
1 teaspoon salt
1 tin chopped tomatoes
½ a vadi
3–4 potatoes, cubed
Small bowl of pakoria
Handful of coriander, chopped

METHOD

To make the tadka (you need very little because the
pakoria and vadi are spicy) heat the oil, put in cumin,
garlic, onion, then fry this for 10–15 minutes on less heat.
Then put in ginger, turmeric, salt, tomatoes and after 5–7
minutes add the vadi, broken up, then potatoes. Then after
10 minutes add boiled water, let it boil till the potato is
nearly ready. Then add the pakoria; they will make the
taree rich, they don't need long, check if they break with a
knife then switch the gas off and add the coriander.

INGREDIENTS

1 ½ cup wholewheat chapati flour
1 ½ cup gram flour
1 teaspoon salt
1 green chilli, finely chopped
1 teaspoon carom seeds
1 onion, diced
1 big spoon ghee
Handful of coriander, chopped

METHOD

Mix all the ingredients in a bowl then use cold water —
slowly, slowly — to make the dough. Take a ball of dough
with your hands, dip it in the dry flour, then roll it out into
a circle (about 3mm thick). Pat the roti in some dry flour
so it doesn't stick. Put the roti on a hot tava, 1 minute on
each side, then put a little bit of oil on both sides and cook
again, both sides, not for too long. With this have butter,
yoghurt and tea.

SHE'S GOT HER WHOLE LIFE, NOW IS HER TIME TO STUDY.

I DON'T WANT HER TO BE STUCK IN THE KITCHEN.

Amanroop: Jasleen's friend

Ian: Jasleen's husband

Mum: Amanroop's mother

Dad: Amanroop's father

Pummy: Jasleen's brother

Bhua: Amanroop's paternal aunt

Sharan: Jasleen's sister

Chacha: Jasleen's paternal uncle

Nani: Jasleen's maternal grandmother,
also referred to as 'Granny'

Massi: Amanroop's maternal aunt

Masur Ji: Amanroop's maternal uncle

My husband's mum: Amanroop's mother-in-law

Me: Amanroop:

---

*At Amanroop's in-laws' house, Southall, London, in
the kitchen cooking aloo parathas for our husbands. She
is rolling the dough and stuffing with potato and I am
cooking them on the taws with olive oil. Amanroop is
comfortable in the kitchen, knows her way around, can do
without thinking too much.*

So everyone has their own aloo recipe?

Yeah, yeah and em, this is my one.
I've added dhaniya, I don't normally
add it but you know, I like dhaniya,
I can add dhaniya in lots of things.
But my 'in-laws here have a different
way of making it where it will be
much spicier, they won't use green
mirch because my brother-in-law
wouldn't eat it.

So they'd use laal mirch?

Yeah, yeah, in everything.

So is that not as good, health-wise?

I don't know you know? I would
assume that, because it's powdered.
But yeah, it's just spicy actually.

Me: Amanroop:

Do the family mind?

No, no.

Okay, so it's not like you are breaking the rules?

No. You know, there are some things
people are really particular about
and then they...they don't like it
when you break it. There are certain
things, but with paratha, as long as
it's spicy enough, it's alright. Because
my mum's family came from Africa,
they have different ways of making
everything. So the kuddi will be
really khati. The spice will be so
much reduced.

What would they put in it, citric acid?

Oh in the kuddi my granny would
just, if she was making kuddi
tomorrow she'd leave the yoghurt
out today so it would just naturally
ferment. Whereas here, it's spicy!
[laughing] Which is fine but when I
cook I like to go back to my roots,

Me: Amanroop:

---

so I go back to how I used to have it when I was a kid. There's this thing called toor de dhal and it's sweet, it's an African Gujarati thing, it's got sugar in it, I'm going to have to make it for you one day.

Do you have it with rice?

You have it with rice, yeah.

[Re-focusing conversation on the cooking at hand] So when you make aloo paratha you fold it in? [dhaniya]

Yeah. We do that with mooli and gobi. And with my aloo I make them tangy with amchoor.

Nice.

Once we went to our friend's house, they made aloo paratha for us and that was the first time I thought about putting amchoor in, because she put amchoor in, but I put far too much citric acid in and nobody could eat them! [laughing] It was funny

because my chacha was over then
from India at the time and he was
really, really polite and he was like, 'it
is a little bit too much.' Amchoor is a
bit safer.

**It's a much rounder flavour, not just tang.
I put it in bhatao.**

I put it in bhatao too.

And I like it in pindia as well.

Hmm, I've done that as well.

Does your dad make sabji then?

My dad? Yeah.

**I think Mum tries to cook for Dad and
my brother, but now that Pummy is
home once a month he always cooks for
himself, I think just to spite to my mum,
because he won't eat her food. That kind
of politics around food is so dark.**

And is that because he doesn't think
it's good for him or...?

Me: Amanroop:

He would say that, but of course that is nonsense. He is a bodybuilder. He wants to 'bulk up,' and all this nonsense, and create his own rules about how much meat he should eat, and all this nonsense, and that didn't fit into what we were eating, so you know, dhal wasn't enough for a person like him. Now he's vegetarian again, but I think he would make up his own eating rules, as and when, just to spite my mum.

To be honest, I feel a lot of our generation is doing that. No dhal; 'Indian food's not healthy, roti's not healthy, so we're gonna eat our own food'...it causes so much tension in families.

Doesn't it?

And you know I went through a phase where I was like, 'yeah, you know roti is so bad actually' but then I learnt that lentils are one of the most alkaline foods you can eat, with so much nutrition! Just have it like you're having soup. You don't need to spend hours cooking because you don't wanna eat Indian food…

Do you want it flipped one more time? [asking about the paratha, making sure I am cooking it the way she and the household like]

Keep it like that for now, just put a bit of oil on it.

It's so interesting that, isn't it?

And it happens in every household. All my cousins are the same you know. But what they do eat instead actually, they don't know what that is. And I think the culture you're brought up in, you know it, and you can make changes. Last week I made kale paneer, so I took palak out of it and put kale in it and I didn't tell anyone! I thought, I want to do this, I want us to be healthy and try different things, but I also want everyone to feel comfortable eating it without saying, 'you have to eat kale because it's good so let's steam it and have it with chicken.'

Me: Amanroop:

I remember Sharan, my sister, saying that. She's married to a Bengali guy and they eat a lot of meat and she made keema with Quorn or soya mince and no one would even know because you're putting that much stuff into it, and because it is a broken up texture, it's not like it's a piece of meat, but yeah nobody would say anything. Do you want oil on the side as well?

> Yeah let's do that.

Yeah, I know what you mean, getting people on your side rather than coming in and saying, 'I know better.'

> Yeah, I remember when I came here, I had never used the pressure cooker — my dad didn't ever have one — he would say, 'no, can't have a pressure cooker. It's better to make it slowly, boil it slowly.' So I came here really anti the pressure cooker.

It's really Punjabi, a pressure cooker.

> Isn't it! Because it saves you gas, it

saves you time and actually when I read into it, it's the best way to cook because the longer you cook something for, the more nutrients will die. Whereas this kind of blitzes it quickly and you retain the nutrients.

And you can use the tharhee as well. Yeah, I've got a pressure cooker, I love it. If I'm ever making dhal, that's what I use, I don't make dhal any other way.

You know what, I've come round to it now, I'm the same. My dad's favourite dhal is maha de dhal and it takes ages to cook.

It's my dad's favourite too.

It's a Punjabi thing. Black dhal, it is the best.

We put black elachi in it and maybe a bit of dhal chini and it's all good! That's my mum's way of doing it. You only put one elachi and one small stick of cinnamon because it's so strong. See if you can get away with that. It's the only way I know

how to make it.

Yeah, it's richer.

Mum does it in a slow cooker. She goes out to work, puts a black dhal on, does the tarka when she gets home, so it's been cooking all day. But I'm scared to leave the slow cooker on. She likes to do it when she's at home too and she can do the housework and things.

Yeah, I make my brown rice in it and everything.

How does brown rice go down in this household?

Well my in-laws don't eat rice, they've never eaten it. It's a roti household. My husband prefers roti to rice as well but he'll have rice occasionally. We have brown rice with things like muttur paneer. And he loves that because it's got this nutty, dense texture and so that works really well. And he always wants us to move towards being healthy, you know

changing to brown atta — small steps
like that.

So last week when my brother was home
they went to my chacha's house and they
use chakki atta, the one that's brown but
looks white. In my mum's house they
use brown atta and my brother had a
big moan saying, 'why don't we use this
atta at home, brown atta has no health
benefits!' Food can be so personal, it can
really hurt people.

Yeah.

So, I started cooking at home to help
my mum out and also because I love
cooking. I used to cook with her as a
child and used to learn by watching,
'okay, how much of this did you put in,
how much of that did you put in?' and
you kind of copy that — get the chance to
make some squint roti. That play, it's part
of learning. And when I got older I'd help
her out, I'd do the cooking some days.
When I moved to London I felt really
homesick and occasionally I'd phone
home and ask, 'Dad, how do you make

**this and Mum, how do you make that?',
phone my nani and ask, 'how do you
make that?' It was more just an excuse
to keep in touch with them. I genuinely
want to record those recipes. Nani told
me how to make her missi roti. It can be
so political. It's not just cooking for the
hell of cooking, it comes with so much
other stuff.**

It really does yeah. Gosh, I mean in
my house I didn't know how to cook
before my mum passed away. My
mum would never let me near the
kitchen, she only taught me how to
gun atta. And make parshaad. That
was it. Nothing else.

What age were you?

I don't remember, maybe I was about
twelve or thirteen? But I had never
rolled a roti, nothing like that. My
gran used to say, 'you should teach
her, she needs to know' and my mum
would say, 'she's got her whole life,
now is her time to study. I don't want
her to be stuck in the kitchen.' And

Me: Amanroop:

---

it's a really big thing in my life, that
my parents, all their focus was on
having a good education because my
dad had done really well at school,
got a scholarship to go and study at
this technical school in Jalandhar. He
left his family at the age of fourteen
to go and live in a boarding school.
He had the top-third result out of the
whole of Punjab! He did amazing, he
did so well! And so he did this BA
and he got this amazing graduate
job in the post office and then got a
chance to join the army and then did
that. Everything in his life was going
up. Then he came here and thought,
'I'm just going to transfer here and
work in a UK post office.' And they
just said, 'you're Asian, you can't
work in the post office.'

What, is that in London? Southall?

Yeah, I think it was in East London.

So all his dreams just...

He had to go and be a labourer. So to

70

this day he says, 'don't set yourself up that you're going to achieve this and that, because you won't be able to in this country.' He really pushed us to have a good education. My mum was also so clever at school, did so well.

Where did she grow up?

Well she was born in Kenya, she went to school in Kenya and when she was thirteen she moved to India and then she came here. She was midway through her A-Levels, she was sixteen when she came here. My grandad said, 'you can't study, because you don't need too much education.' So he just got her a job in a factory somewhere.

Do you know which one?

I don't remember any of this, it was my massi who told my brother a few months ago, 'did you know Mum worked in a factory?' It was either in a button factory or a safety-pin factory or something like that. It

was one of those things, something
really small. I had no idea my mum
worked in a factory. She was so clever
but my grandad didn't let her, or my
oldest massi, study more than just
the basics. And my massi is nearly
sixty-five and ever since she got here,
she's been doing these accountancy
courses. She's about to retire but she's
still doing exams. And we all said to
her, 'why don't you stop, what are you
gonna do with them now?' and she
said, 'well my dad didn't let me study
and I'm going to study now, until I
die.'

Where does she do them?

She does them online, home courses
where you study for a module and
then you sit the exam. What could
she and my mum have been if they
had actually done what they wanted
to? Mum never let me in the kitchen
and then when she died, everyone was
just panicked, they were like, 'Roopi
doesn't know how to cook! What are
they going to do?' But my dad knew

how to cook because he lived on his own sincc he was fourteen, so he knew how to cook everything, you know, dhal, roti, everything. Even sometimes when we were little and when Mum would take us swimming sometimes, we would come home and my dad…

Your mum took you swimming?

Yeah, yeah. Every Friday we'd go swimming.

That's so un-Punjabi! So you can swim?

We would come home and my dad would have made dhal for us. It was this equal home where my dad never wanted to take my mum for granted — that's to say, 'she should be cooking and I should be putting my feet up.' He was a skilled carpenter, doing a physical job and he didn't think, 'well I should put my feet up.' So I think my brother and I got that from them and how they both grew up. So when she died we

had just moved house, we moved
to Hayes, into this huge house that
my mum dreamt of. It was really
far away from our school, so my
dad had to give up his job to take
us. He was so miserable, I mean of
course, he didn't know what to do in
life! You know they'd just invested
into this huge property and it was a
shell. We had no kitchen, we had no
cupboards, nothing. We were living
out of suitcases and boxes, we had no
carpets, nothing.

Was your dad going to do it up then?

He was going to be doing it up yeah,
at the weekends. And then six months
later she died, yeah.

How did she die?

She had been suffering headaches
for months and the doctor had
said, 'you're just stressed out.' But
actually she had had a blockage in
her head, It was a cyst and em…it
just wasn't found in time. And she'd

gone to hospital — she'd never been
to hospital in her life except to have
us — so she went into hospital and
they gave her sleeping pills and so she
slept that night and in the morning
woke up, had a cup of tea and just
collapsed because pressure had built
up. None of us were there. Me and
my brother went to school and he kept
saying, 'I don't want to go to school,
I want to go to the hospital, I want to
see Mum.' At break we went to the
reception and Masur Ji was there, he
had been there for an hour and they
hadn't let him take us because he
wasn't on their list. We said, 'he's our
uncle, it's fine, our mum's in hospital.'
The whole journey he didn't tell us
anything, he just said, 'oh your mum
just wants to speak to you.' [laughing
unbelievably] We went to the hospital
and they said, 'oh she's unconscious'
[she pauses] and…um… that's it, 'you
can go and see her if you want.' And
we went to see her and they didn't
know what was wrong, I had no clue
what to say, I was just silent! Then
after that they moved her to a hospital

in Wimbledon. Half of the family went home cause they were like, 'yeah she's going to be fine there.'

So she was in a coma?

Yeah, she was in a coma. She was on life support. So we went to the other hospital and they'd operated. The surgeon just came and said, 'I'm sorry, it's too late, she's going to die. You can say your goodbyes and everything but once you've done that we're going to have to turn the life support off because her brain is dead.' So yeah, that was that...

Then we came home and I remember my massi, because we hadn't eaten all day, she made us this toast with jam on it and put it in front of me and it was the first time I'd ever said no to food — I didn't have a hunger. And my bhua stayed with us for two weeks or something like that. She would come and sleep with us because she was like, you know, 'how are you guys going to live?' And she would cook for

us and clean the house for us.
She would come and say, 'look, watch
me make dhal, watch me make this,
watch me make that...' Everyone
would come over and bring food.
Every Sunday, my massi would come
with a huge pot of chicken and sabji
and dhals and would say, 'here, this
is going to get you through the week.'
For months we got though like that.

Cooking?

It would be cooking and just sitting
together, eating together. I think my
dad appreciated that he didn't have to
think about it.

Did anyone else help with the cooking when you moved in with your husband's family? Your massis or your husband?

Nobody, no one. My husband was
great, I am honestly so blessed
because he's allowed me space.
When I first got married, when all
the family left, all the family that had
come from India, I got a new job and

started to work from home. I would work from my dad's house because at my husband's family home the laptop didn't connect to the internet. So every Thursday I'd go and sit at my dad's house and talk to him and I would make him something. I would make a pot of dhal or make sabji or something to last him a few days so he wouldn't have to worry, or I would take something from home. And I would wash the clothes, if I could see clothes around I would just wash them. Things like that, I would just end up doing... My huband's mum is an angel. She always says to me, 'why don't you go and give some sabji to your dad? Why don't you go and do this for your dad, why don't you go and do that?' And she tells me I don't go over enough, 'why don't you call him here one day and he can have dinner with us?'

And does he?

He does come yeah. He's very shy because he thinks, 'she's at her in-laws, I shouldn't go over too much.'

Me: Amanroop:

That old traditional thing. In a White British community you don't necessarily live with your in-laws and I see a lot of our friends and Ian's parent's friends worrying and caring for their parents — that's a universal worry isn't it? You want to be there to look after them and it's such a burden and they don't want to be a burden, but you want to look after them.

I was just going to check how many we've got? [parathas]

Probably a lot. Gosh they're hot! Eh, two, four, six, eight, ten.

We'll make a couple more.

How did you feel coming into this house with a sister-in-law cooking and a new kitchen to navigate?

I don't like this kitchen. Back at my dad's house, we'd be talking, watching the same programme on TV and I'd cook at the same time.

Me: Amanroop:

My sister-in-law was at home on
maternity leave, she'd just had a baby,
and everything would be done by
the time I got home. The roti, dhal,
everything would be made and I
would just help her make the roti's
like we are now. The kitchen is where
I'm creative. My husband and my
brother always laugh at me because
sometimes I make something really
nice and then the second time I make
it, it doesn't taste the same and it's
because I've changed it. For me it's
my creativity and I don't want to
just follow the same recipe. I want
to add a bit of meaning to it or add
something different.

**I just love a simple yellow dhal, I could
eat it every night of the week.**

It's the same as soup, you don't have
to waste your time thinking about
what to cook, you just put the dhal on.

**And it's so nourishing and filling and
always tastes better the second day. Ian
calls it, 'second-day dhal'. Occasionally**

Me: Amanroop:

---

if Dad was out at the Gurdwara or
something, me and my mum would have
dhal and chips.

I've never had that.

Forget roti just have some oven chips on
the side. Sometimes you'd dip 'em in.

I wonder, back in Punjab, back in the day,
whether there was anyone innovating,
growing new things? Or, something
wouldn't grow that year so they'd use
something else. When we've come over
here, it means so much over here, it's
your heritage, you eat your heritage,
you're eating your culture every night.
It's so important, it's how you remember,
how you sustain, how you feel a certain
way, it's your tongue, it's your taste, it's
everything — but I wonder whether we
hold on to it more because we're not
there?

It's really interesting being with someone
who's not from an Indian background, not
from a Punjabi household and what then I
choose to...

Me: Amanroop:

---

*WHAT
YOU CHOOSE TO KEEP HOLD OF
/
PRACTICE IN YOUR OWN LIFE. BE IT
COOKING A CURRY, READING
A PRAYER...*

*AS A SIKH WOMAN WHO HAS MARRIED
A NON-SIKH, BRITISH MAN, I FEEL LIKE I
AM PITIED. 'OH HOW WILL SHE BRING UP
HER CHILDREN AS SIKH, SHE CAN'T BE
SIKH?' AND I SAY, 'WELL ACTUALLY I AM'*

*— WHAT WOULD PATRIARCHAL
CULTURE/RELIGION LOOK LIKE IF
WOMEN HAD A VOICE?*

**Your food is so much a part of that and
it's so nice that it's something you can
share with everyone. I remember the
first time I went to Ian's family home, I
made aloo paratha for breakfast and they
were just, 'wow, this is unbelievable,
you can stay!' It is something you can
share, everyone gets it, it's universal. It's
inclusive because everyone eats.**

Me:　　　Amanroop:

IT IS STRANGE THAT I SAID THIS,
BECAUSE I HAD AN EATING DISORDER
FOR ALMOST HALF MY LIFE.

Put 6 large handfuls of oily toor di dhal in a bowl and soak in hot water for 15 minutes. Wash thoroughly, rubbing off the oil with your fingers, and rinse in cold water.

Add the washed dhal to a large pot filled 2/3 to the top with hot water and 1 ½ teaspoon of salt. Bring to the boil, reduce heat and cook for 45 minutes until the dhal is soft and combined (the lentils should still retain their shape but should be a more soupy consistency).

Heat 2 tablespoons of butter/ghee in a pan and add 1 tablespoon of rai. When hot, the rai will start popping. Once popped, reduce heat and add 4 large chopped tomatoes with the skins removed (to do this place the whole tomatoes into a large pan of boiled water for about 5 minutes, the skin will start to split and you'll be able to peel it off). Add 1/3 teaspoon of haldi, 1 or 2 chillies (depending on how spicy you like it), 1 teaspoon of salt and 1–1 ½ serving spoons of brown sugar, depending on how sweet you like it!

Once the tomatoes have broken down, add the thurka to the dhal and serve with plain boiled rice.

I learnt to make parshaad using semolina but in the
Gurdwara it is made using wheat flour (atta). The rest of
the ingredients are the same.

Melt ½ a cup of butter or ghee in a pan. Add 1 cup
of semolina and cook slowly on a low flame, stirring
continuously, until the semolina is cooked and is light
brown in colour. This will take 5–10 minutes but don't
stop stirring, as the semolina will burn. If the mixture
looks dry add a few more tablespoons of butter. It should
resemble wet sand. Add 1 cup of white sugar and then,
very carefully, add 3 cups of boiling water whilst mixing
continuously. The mixture will bubble at first but keep
stirring until the mixture combines and comes away from
the edges. Eat while hot.

You can garnish the parshaad with raisins, coconut or
almond flakes if you like.

A SHOPPING LIST

1 Oil Spray
1 Chopping Board
1 Pizza Cutter
1 Ice Cream Scoop
12 million people displaced
1 million died
75,000 women raped, kidnapped, abducted

All together

WELL YOU'RE THE ONE FEEDING THEM, EVERY WEEK, ALL OF THEM.

Mireille: Jasleen's studio mate

Bolly: Mireille's mother, Edna's aunt

Edna: Bolly's niece

Nikita: Edna's daughter

Bolly's mum: Mireille's grandmother

Bolly's dad: Mireille's grandfather

Christine: Bolly's sister

Elsie: Edna's mother

Bismark: Bolly's brother

Jules: Edna's brother

Jonathan: Jules' son, Edna's nephew

Francis: Edna's husband

Tanmeet: Jasleen's cousin

Bob: Bolly's husband

Me: Mireille: Bolly: Edna: Nikita:

At Mireille's family home in Balham, London with
Bolly, Edna and Nikita, eating take-away and
homemade fish cakes.

I went from Goa to the Middle
East when I was nineteen.

What took you there?

It was kind of, my parents died,
nothing to stay for. [weeping]

So both your parents had died by the time
you were…

One died when I was fifteen.

How did they pass away?

She was sick, Mum. And Dad
died from drinking very heavy.
Very heavy.

I used to tell him, 'Dad don't do
that, we are here too.'

When Mum died I was fifteen.
Mum was always sick, she

had a heart problem and Dad
spent lots of money on her,
like you know, put her in a
hospital, make her better. I
think it was also something to
do with her kidney, probably,
kidney and heart. And when
Dad was drinking heavy, heavy,
heavy, his liver went, cirrhosis,
whatever it is.

What happened in the house after that?

Dad was in Bombay, he was
working on the ships in music,
he used to play violin. Every
two years he used to come
home. I never thought my dad
would go [die] so quickly.
When we buried Mum, all the
men were talking and one of
them said, 'oh my god you've
got two years to live' to my
dad. We'd just buried our mum,
just buried our mum! Imagine,
listening to that. News that he's
going to die in two years' time.

If he didn't stop drinking?

> Yeah. His liver was gone
> completely. The doctor gave
> him two years so he went to
> Delhi, all that, and then that's
> it, two years after Mum, he
> died. So when I was nineteen
> I just went to the Middle East.
> Getting away, from everything.
>
> You know how it is in India,
> you don't get benefits. You have
> to survive. I said to my sister,
> 'I have to earn the money.' So
> I was doing babysitting, like a
> nanny, then I worked with the
> Kuwait Embassy and they took
> me to the Middle East. I was
> very young.
>
> > Brave.

Yeah.

> When I was there, my boss
> said, 'now you're going to go
> to England with my daughter

because she's expecting the
baby.' She took me to Lebanon,
I went there, I came here to
England, I went back to India
and then I came back here.

**So when you came here with the woman
who was pregnant, where did you end
up?**

St John's Wood, I used to live
there. A lot of Arabs live there.
Rich, rich people.

Did you ever feel homesick?

Of course I did. But I had no
choice darling. I didn't have
no choice. I had to get one
hundred rupees to India. I used
to send fifty rupees to my sister
Christine, and fifty rupees for
me.

Did you want to get married?

I didn't know anybody there!
My boss wanted to arrange a
marriage for me, but I didn't

know that man. He was Goan,
but what can I say, I didn't
know him very well. I said, 'no
please don't do that, if I want
to get married, I get married
who I want to.' I had a hard life
darling. Very hard life. And you
know what, when I was working,
the Punjabi people doesn't
respect me in Delhi! They don't
respect you!

Really. Why do you think that was?

Because I'm not married! I'm not
married and I'm working!

Because you're the lower-class worker?

Yeah!

Yeah, I've seen that myself, it's horrible.

When I was living in a flat with
others, one of the boys tried to
rape me and his mother said,
'you have to get rid of that girl,
she's no good, she's not married.'

95

Me: Mireille: Bolly: Edna: Nikita:

Where's that Bolly, here?

In Delhi.

So this is when you were nannying in Delhi?

Yeah, yeah, in 1966, they didn't like people like that.

Do you remember what area of Delhi?

Jangpura.

In Goa we were quite well-off, in our own way. You know how India has the caste system? You cannot talk about India without mentioning it. We were quite a high caste, we were not Brahmins, we were the next ones, so we were quite high up. In Goa we've got our own status. Even though we

96

are poor, we are still, even if the house is destroyed, it's who you *are* in Goa.

What does that mean?

Like the surnames mean quite a lot, so you're from a wealthy family, so you could be poor and have nothing to eat but that surname just holds you up. But when we went to Delhi everything changed, because in Delhi you've got the Punjabis, you've got the rich Indians, you've got the Sikhs. And Goans were, because they were half-Portuguese, they have no identity in Delhi. 'Who are you? You're not Indian, you're not true Indian, you've got Portuguese

blood in you.' So you're
a nobody.

Some of our Goan
girls would fall in love
with Punjabi boys. It
was just, 'no way, we
are Punjabis, there is
no way a Goan girl
can join our family.'
We were like Anglo-
Indians, almost treated
like half of something.
They were like, 'they're
Portuguese, they
drink, they eat meat,
they dance, they wear
dresses.' If she [to
Bolly] wore a dress and
walked on the street
she would get a slap
on her arse. Literally,
I have seen it, or they
pull your hair.

I was raped nearly, by students,
they ganged me. In Delhi, the
worst place, I tell you. If my

friend Frankie wasn't there,
I would have been raped by
a gang.

**So you were an object, they could
do whatever, and no one would say
anything.**

But Delhi is still like
that, still got that
mentality. Not with
Goans now, it's just
generally like that.

Did you say your mum worked in Delhi?

No, just a pure
housewife. Dad, he
worked a lot and that
too I realised, only
recently, when I sat
down with him and
said, 'how much did
you earn?' And he
earned then, what
people earn now.

Do you think that was quite a pivotal

thing for the family then?

Yeah he was the main man on their side, almost to the point that when my mother died she said to my dad, 'make sure you keep an eye on them,' so I think he took that responsibility literally on board.

Oh yeah, he wrote a letter to my brother-in-law, Edna's dad, 'look after my children' because he knew he was dying, he put us in the debts. Property was going…

So your parents put you in debt?

Yeah. We had a big house, big land, it was going for auction because both were sick, really sick, probably spent all the money, Mum's gold, everything was gone.

Me: Mireille: Bolly: Edna: Nikita:

MY BROTHER SOLD MY MUM'S GOLD WITHOUT HER KNOWING. I DON'T KNOW WHAT HE USED THE MONEY FOR. WHEN I GOT MARRIED, MY GRANNY TRADED IN TWO GOLD KURAY FOR TWO NEW ONES FOR ME. GOLD SIGNIFIES MUCH MORE THAN A GIFT, IT'S THE HANGOVER FROM A DOWRY.

Do you know how these debts came to be?

You know what happened, he started building a house, your grandfather, [to Mireille] her [Bolly's] dad. It was a big house, but it never got completed, so I think when you built a house there, you borrow money - he earned a lot of money, he was the best earner. But a lot of money was wasted because Bolly's mother gave it away to her family, to her brothers,

her sisters, whatever
money her father sent.

You know sometimes I think
I wouldn't be here, you know
what I mean? If we had lots of
money saved somewhere. We
had the money but I think poor
Mum used to be bullied by her
sisters and her sister's husband.

He opened his own
business, he used all
their money.

They cheated us a lot. Cheated
us a lot! And then you know,
when you don't have money,
then her [Edna's] dad helped to
keep the house. Her dad put up
the money, it was going in the
auction. When her dad save our
property and everything, I had
to pay him back, so I worked
hard darling, all my life and I
paid my debts, my dad's debts.

Did you pay them all off?

Me: Mireille: Bolly: Edna: Nikita:

Yes!

Wow.

I paid all the debts of my dad,
and who got the property now?
My brother. My brother got
the property, he got the field,
everything.

It's painful actually, it's really painful.
[to Edna]

They're well off.
Properties and
everything, they're
quite well off.

So what's happened with that land?

It's still there, it's his.

Now it's very much his.

And do you speak with him?

I speak with him, but what can
I say.

Me: Mireille: Bolly: Edna: Nikita:

Something strikes me, and I feel like I'm saying this because it's my own experience as well, but the women, in general and of the family, are never treated anywhere near as well as the men of the family are treated.

You are right.

You are right. It's like a thread going through.

Do you have brothers Edna?

I have one brother.

They're very close!

They're very close!

It's nice.

I make it my business to be close. That's the funny thing about me because I don't want ever to feel in my life that I have not done my best for…you know…I love my family. Also on my father's side, his sisters, I am very close with them too. It just comes naturally, I want to help, I want to do, it's 'seva.'

What is that word, what is it?

It's serving.

It's like selfless serving. Doing something, without expecting anything back. But that word resonates with me, because I've been brought up with it as well in the Gurdwara…

Yeah, you all are very much into that, that's the essence of being who you are.

Yeah, definitely, but there's something about it here, where I feel like [pause] you can't keep giving. When do you stop?

Yeah, this is where I am at the moment.

As a woman, providing, nourishing for everybody...how do you self-care?

[to Edna] But you said this literally before Jasleen came through the door.

I'm at that point in my life, I think it's because I'm reaching my sixtieth birthday next year, I think it's all coming together for me and I think, at what point...? Because I serve my church quite a lot, physically serving my church, and I pray three to four hours a day, I'm into prayer. I pray from three o'clock in the morning.

Does that keep you strong?

Yeah. Because

sometimes I amaze myself and I think, 'wow, how do you do it?' And it's not me, it's something from above, it's something from above. But also, at the same time, I am thinking, you know, 'when?'…Because I cook for Jules, I've cooked for him for twenty years now, my brother.

You cook for Jules?

For twenty years I've been cooking.

Okay, so how do you fit that in? Do you work too?

Yeah I work. I work, I cook, I look after my family, I look after my parents.

Me: Mireille: Bolly: Edna: Nikita:

When do you fit in cooking for Jules? [laughing unbelievably]

How many years you cooking for him now?

Twenty, twenty years. Since his wife has gone, I've taken it on.

How did you take on that role, did you offer, or feel sorry for him?

For me, my flesh and blood… If I've got food on the table and my flesh and blood is a couple of streets away from me, not experiencing that because they haven't got a wife or a mother, because Jonathan was only seven, I could not eat that food. And that's where it comes from for me. It really comes from that deep

sense of family — I
love my family, I love
them so much, I don't
even think they realise
how much I love them?

Does that hurt?

Yeah, the love hurts
so much because now
that I'm getting old,
I'm quite feeble, I'm
getting frail and my life
is slowing down. But
that's where it comes
from, it comes from
deep-within love. But
it is for everybody, first
my family, but it is also
for everybody else.

**So when you would cook for your brother
and his son would you go there, would
they come to you?**

No, they would come
to pick the food up.
He still comes on

Me: Mireille: Bolly: Edna: Nikita:

Sunday…

Every Sunday.

…I fill a bag…

Every Sunday.

Every Sunday,
every Sunday.

I had no idea this was going on!

Yeah! Edna cooks for him so
many years now.

**So what time do you start on a Sunday
morning?**

Well, I start preparing
on a Thursday evening,
I prepare all my spices,
all my wet spices, my
masalas I make fresh. It's
to a point now it's like
a menu, 'what are we
cooking this weekend?'

It's like a
restaurant.

So I'll say to Francis,
'get me three kilos
of mutton, two kilos
of pork, two kilos of
mince, vegetables,
dhals,' it's never less
than two kilos. And
Jonathan likes snack
foods so I'd be very
aware of that, so I
make him fish cakes,
not every week but
I'll try fit that in, or
tandoori chicken,
spiced chicken…

Your brother, does he say thank you?

I think I see it in a…he
will not say thank you
but he knows. Deep
down he knows.

**So you are kind of filling in this mother
role, or wife role.**

With all of them, I am
as a mother, but with
him as a wife. Because
I do everything for my
parents, I look after
that house to a certain
degree, the house in
Goa.

**You remind me of my cousin Tanmeet.
She's younger than me, so she's my
massi and my chacha's daughter. So my
dad's brother got married to my mum's
sister, and I have two cousins, both girls
and Tanmeet is the eldest. I go to her
for everything. But I'm also really aware
that she needs to look after herself, you
know? She can't always look after me.**

Do you want some tea?

Diwali! Have some mittah.
Happy Diwali!

**I will! I'd love a tea. Your husband, is he
White British?**

He's from Goa but he

112

came here to study. He
was so Westernised and
I was so Indian because
I'd just come from
India. I was eighteen
when I came, met him
when I was twenty-one.

Are you still together?

[tentatively] Yeah, yeah,
yeah. Often not, but we
are together! We are
content.

Content is the
word.

You know, we are
getting old together.

Jas got married recently!

Not to an Indian man. A White British man.

Where did you meet
him?

Me: Mireille: Bolly: Edna: Nikita:

At the Royal College of Art. At art school. He's one of the best men I have ever met, and I guess...yeah...I've been thinking a lot about, that that's no surprise...

FINDING FRIENDSHIP OR LOVE IN A MAN THAT HAS OPPOSITE TRAITS TO THE MEN THAT I GREW UP WITH.

[To Bolly] When you got married to Bob, was it a problem? Did people think, 'why are you marrying a non-Goan?'

No, because I didn't have parents, I didn't care, I just got married darling. I just got registered married and we still living in this flat, Mireille is born and I'm still here!

It's nice tea, is it cardamom?

It's a chai.

It's a chai oh, Indian, Indian.

Me: Mireille: Bolly: Edna: Nikita:

But you know it's from Sainsbury's, it's a really good brand. Did you want tea? [to Bolly]

No, no, I'll have some warm water.

Is this like punjeeri in here?

Yeah that's a Goan sweet.

What do you call it?

Neurio. Did you like my fish cakes?

You made them? They were the best things on the plate! Which fish were they, salmon?

Mackerel, fresh mackerel.

I learnt from her.

So the fish cakes were homemade, the pickle was homemade?

The best stuff was homemade.

I often think about the background that my dad comes from like, poverty, and I've been recently reading this book about Partition.

Me: Mireille: Bolly: Edna: Nikita:

Oh I've been watching
all of the programmes.

Was your dad already in
Pakistan, was he already in
Punjab?

**No, he wasn't born when it was Partition
but I think about... so he told me a story
years ago about family friends of his
that mark their wives and daughters
lives because at Partition, a lot of people
were killing their own wives and own
daughters because they didn't want them
to be raped or abducted.**

So they killed
them?

Yeah, yeah, they would rape the
girls.

Hang on, hang on a minute. Let me get
this straight, people were...

Men.

Men were killing their own women?

116

Me: Mireille: Bolly: Edna: Nikita:

Because women's bodies were instrumentalised, they were used, and I just think…'this is what we come from.' My dad, when he tells me this story, he says it's izzat — it's duty.

They would rather kill them themselves and not have to go through that shame of having their daughters or wives being raped.

Also the British did not help them much.

No! They just drew the line, they didn't expect anyone to move *en mass*.

In terms of like female heritage and legacy, to be so submissive that you're used as a kind of pawn, you're a pawn in all of this aren't you?

Yeah.

Women are.

Me: Mireille: Bolly: Edna: Nikita:

But I think your dad is very
wrong to say that.

**It's the mindset isn't it. It's always
decided by the men.**

Even though we are
quite strong women,
strong, strong, strong.

Well you're the one feeding them, every
week, all of them.

Fish Cutlets

INGREDIENTS

1 mackerel (steam the mackerel,
take out the bones, leave to cool)
1 large onion, cut very fine
2 tins tuna fish in oil, drained

METHOD

Mix the onion, tuna, mackerel
and 2 small boiled and peeled
potatoes with:

Lots of black pepper
Pinch of cinnamon powder
Pinch of clove powder
Pinch of jeera
Little green chilli (optional)
Add a little lemon juice and a little malt vinegar

Mix and put in fridge to harden.

Make round cakes from the mix.
Coat in fine semolina. Slowly fry, not too much,
on slow fire.

INGREDIENTS

For the masala:
5 teaspoons chilli powder
1 ½ teaspoons coriander
½ teaspoon cumin
½ teaspoon turmeric
1 onion
1 green chilli (fat not long)
5 tablespoons Maggi
coconut powder
Walnut-size piece of
tamarind (from a block
soaked in a cup of boiling
water, squeeze and chuck
the pulp once soaked, make
sure no seeds are present
when grinding)
2 sola (also known as
kokum or bhirand —
a Goan souring agent)

For the curry:
Handful of okra
Prawns (however many are
in the pack, if you can get
them with the heads still on
even better)
1 onion
1 green chilli (fat not long)

METHOD

For the masala, soak
tamarind and 2 sola in
water (1 hour), meanwhile
grind all dry masala
ingredients with the onion,
chilli and coconut powder.
Blend with soaked tamarind
and sola, adding soaking
liquid to loosen.

For the curry, poach the
okra and set aside. Fry the
onion and green chilli then
remove and set aside. In the
same pan fry the prawns
and add the masala paste,
loosen with a little water.
Now add the poached okra,
fried onions and chilli.

[Eaten with sliced
white in Mickey's camp
kitchen, Easter, 2015, near
Sherringham.]

Amanprit Sandhu

THE FEEÐER AND FEEÐING

_a parallel text

Feeder
(fee-der)
Noun
a person or thing that supplies food
or feeds something.

Amanprit Sandhu

My beloved Harbans, the breadbasket of India is dying, and the five rivers are contaminated and running dry. High as a kite. I don't know this land anymore — its smells, noises, tastes and rumblings are foreign to me. And even if I did, I don't know if I could return. I am twice displaced. Today I spent some time by our water well in the village. I sat silently for an hour, listening, and waiting for the wind to bring back to me the sound of my mother's husky voice and her heavy footsteps. She'd bring roti and lassi to us every day whilst we worked out in the fields. For a moment it all came back, filled and nourished me. But memories cannot be our only sustenance and who cares for them anyway now.

Ajit. Thank you. For your message. I'm watching the Phulkari programme on the Sangat TV and they are discussing how to make whole milk lassi, the old-fashioned way. And you know this classical Punjabi culture is told by women just like me. They always listen to the dukh sukh (sadness and happiness) of the ladies that phone in. And it gives me great comfort to hear the stories of these women, as they are my stories too, our stories. Please finish the paperwork for the land and return to us quickly. Yours, Harbans.

A fictional conversation between Ajit and Harbans, a first-generation couple who moved from the Punjab to the UK.

In 1978 writer and activist Amrit Wilson
published the first edition of *Finding a Voice: Asian
Women in Britain*. The book presented first-hand
accounts of South Asian women's lives and
struggles through interviews and discussions.
The book gave voice to the experience of being a
migrant, a worker, and a woman in 1970s Britain.
It wrote South Asian women into the working
class struggles and the key events of the time
through their own words and highlighted their
contributions. Within Wilson's seminal book,
rewriting and reclaiming her-stories were not just
the domain of middle-class 'revolutionaries' or
liberal thinkers.

'My body is broken today…who will cook for me
when I'm older?'

Based in the cold foods section my mother, on
an average working day, prepares 600 trays
of food within seven hours for in-flight meals.
Over 100 migrant workers from South Asian,
Romanian and Polish backgrounds feed hundreds
of travellers flying from London Heathrow to
Cape Town, Hong Kong, Berlin, Chicago, Mexico
City…Whenever I fly, I think of them all — it is
the only time I bless and give thanks for my food.

123

Sometimes when we eat together at home, my mother tells me stories about co-workers and in turn implicitly reveals her own fears. Always delivered in a deadpan and matter-of-fact way, there is the story of the co-worker who suffered a massive heart attack in the toilet, after clocking off from a double shift. The woman whose adult children couldn't pay for her funeral as they were all financially dependent on her. Women with physical ailments requesting more overtime to pay for new items for their semi-detached house, or a lavish wedding for their daughter or son.

Many of the women from my mother's generation are now in their sixties and have worked throughout their lives, whilst simultaneously running a household, looking after children and cooking. The labour involved in feeding and its impact on their bodies coexists and is sometimes at odds with the romanticised idea of the South Asian mother and dutiful feeder. In turn the relationship to food, domestic life and working life is personal, social and political in unexpected ways for all involved.

In 2005 South Asian migrant workers employed
by the catering firm Gate Gourmet entered a
dispute with their employers. In the late 1990s
in-flight meal preparations were outsourced to
Gate Gourmet from British Airways at Heathrow
Airport. Changes to the terms and conditions
of workers' employment contracts ensued. Less
sick pay, a reduction in the money received for
working overtime and shorter breaks all led to the
women striking.

Gate Gourmet's work force at the time was
predominately made up of Punjabi Sikh women
who lived in the nearby areas of Southall,
Hounslow and Heston, London. The proximity
to Heathrow Airport made it a major source
of employment for migrants. Speaking little
English and predominately only having only been
educated to Year Eleven in India, the women were
classed as unskilled workers and often took low
paid jobs involving some form of manual labour.

Whilst the Grunwick dispute at Grunwick Film Processing Laboratories in the 1970s (dubbed the 'strikers in saris') was propelled into the media spotlight with marches organised in solidarity with the Indian women, with some eventual support from the trade unions, the political landscape in Britain and its workers had changed significantly by 2005.

The press that the Punjabi Sikh strikers received instead emphasised the delays caused to travellers and the money lost. And their own union were unable to support them fully. Whilst many of those involved in the strikes eventually went back to work for the company, a number of women lost their jobs and were replaced by agency workers. Their requests half met. These women formed part of British labour history and their stories are still to be told.

Perhaps the strongest form of protest for a South Asian woman is to not be a feeder, or to not feed herself or others on time. To hate the smell of raw and cooked ingredients, to ignore well preserved cooking methods and hand-me-down recipes.

And to re-evaluate the tastes, stories and
memories we have been told to hold dear to us.

To not feed on the pain and his-stories of others,
and to not feed one's self for a collective cause.

Hunger Strike — a refusal to eat food.
Often undertaken as a form of protest.

Jayaben Desai, the leading figure of the Grunwick
dispute, held a hunger strike outside the TUC
headquarters in November 1977. Short lived and
having minimum impact within the context of
their wider campaign, the female hunger striker
remains a powerful symbol of resistance often
marginalised within history. Suffragette prisoners
often adopted the hunger strike whilst in prison
and were violently force-fed.

The IRA hunger strikes of the 1980s involved
many women who are largely unknown. More
recently and poignantly in February 2018
more than 100 refugee women at Yarl's Wood
Immigration Removal Centre undertook a hunger
strike over their severe living conditions at the
facility.

'Wife beats up man for asking for more rotis'
—Ahmedabad Mirror, Oct 11, 2014.

The following are ingredients required for makki ki roti, a favourite and staple of any Punjabi cuisine. Serves 4 people. Cooking time: minutes.

FOR THE MAIN DISH

1 cup maize flour
1 pinch red chilli powder
boiling water as required
1 ½ tablespoon ghee
½ teaspoon salt

1 handful finely chopped
fenugreek leaves (methi)
1 tablespoon butter

Note: This text is one-third fiction, one-third historical and one-third autobiographical. My her-stories, memories and fictions are built on the fulkari shoulders of many women including Bishan Kaur, Harbans Kaur, Gurmeet Kaur and Narinder Kaur.